WILLIAM'S HOUSE

For Jim and Jimmy Redmond, always ready with hammer and nails—G.H.

For Melanie, Andrew, and Peter—L.D.

Published by The Millbrook Press, Inc.
2 Old New Milford Road
Brookfield, CT 06804
www.millbrookpress.com

Text copyright © 2001 by Ginger Howard
Illustrations copyright © 2001 by Larry Day

Printed in the United States of America
5 4 3 2 1

Library of Congress Cataloging-in-Publication Data
Howard, Ginger.
William's House / Ginger Howard ; Illustrated by Larry Day.
p. cm.
Summary: Arriving in New England in 1637, William is determined to recreate his home in England but realizes that climate requires modifications to it.
ISBN 0-7613-1674-4 (lib. bdg.)
[1. Dwellings—Fiction. 2. New England—History—Colonial period, ca. 1600-1775—Fiction.]
I. Day, Larry, 1956- ill. II. Title
PZ7.H83287 Wi   2001 [E]—dc21   99-057296

WILLIAM'S HOUSE

by

Ginger Howard

Illustrated by Larry Day

The Millbrook Press
Brookfield, Connecticut

NEW ENGLAND, 1637

William knew just the kind of house he wanted. It would be like the house he grew up in, his father's house, in England.

William cleared an area 20 feet square. He used the felled trees for the upright posts. The saplings were used for the fence. Then he went to the woods and cut rafters to hold the thatch roof. He split planks for clapboards. And he fashioned wood pegs to hold everything in place.

William's wife, Elizabeth, wanted a window, but William had no glass. He scraped a piece of animal horn until it was translucent. Then he made a wide slit in the clapboards, and covered the opening with the horn.

William used clay and stones from the creek bed to build a small fireplace in one corner of the room. He placed two pegs on the wall, one for his extra shirt, and one for his wife's apron. Then he made a board table with the side of a packing crate. And finally, he stuffed bags with corn husks for beds.

When all was done, William and Elizabeth and their two sons sat at the board. They dipped their fingers into trenchers of pudding and bread. A noggin of cider was passed from hand to hand. After supper, they folded their long napkins and put them in the chest.

As soon as it was dark, William covered the glowing embers with ashes. William and his wife climbed into bed, and the boys climbed onto the table to sleep. William smiled. He thought of the new house, and it was just like the one he grew up in, his father's house, in England.

The days grew longer, and soon it was summer.

"It is hotter here than at home in England," said William.

The barrels of pork began to spoil, and the root vegetables began to sprout.

"Something must be done," said his wife, "or we'll have no food!"

So William dug a hole deep in the cool earth behind the house. He moved the barrels and the vegetables into the new cellar.

In August, the winds started to blow.

"It is windier here than at home in England," said William.

A strong gust blew a tree down near the house.

"Something must be done," said his wife, "or we'll be crushed!"

So William cut away the trees and left a large clearing all around the house.

By mid-October, the reds and oranges of autumn had turned to browns.

"It is drier here than at home in England," said William.

The sparks from the chimney landed on the dry thatch, and the roof began to smolder.

"Something must be done," said his wife, "or the house will burn!"

So William split shingles of cedar and replaced the thatch on the roof.

By late November, the days were short and gray.

"There is more snow here than at home in England," said William.

The snow piled higher and higher on the roof until the rafters sagged with the weight.

"Something must be done," said his wife, "or the roof will cave in!"

So William cleared the snow and removed the shingles. He built a new roof with a very steep pitch and replaced the shingles.

In January, the days were the bleakest of all.

"It is colder here than at home in England," said William.

The boys could not move their toes when they woke in the morning, and the dog could not wag his tail.

"Something must be done," said his wife, "or we'll freeze in our sleep!"

So William built a new fireplace, wider and taller, in the center of the wall.

One day, the sun was strong enough to melt the frozen crust on the newly formed buds. Spring had arrived. And with it, a ship from England sailed into the harbor.

Familiar voices calling through the trees brought a quick halt to the family's work. William's face lit up as he, Elizabeth, and the boys all ran to greet Cousin Samuel and his wife, Constance. There were hugs and laughs and bursts of news and even more hugs.

And then, Cousin Samuel turned toward the clearing.
"What kind of house is this?" he asked.

William turned also and took a long look at the house. The window was a piece of animal horn. The food was in a cellar. The house stood in a clearing. The roof was very steep and made of shingles. The fireplace was large and in the center of the wall. The house did not look like his father's house in England.

William looked at his wife.
Then he turned to his cousin and answered,
"This is our new home. Welcome!"

They all went inside. The adults sat above the salt and the children stood below. They shared trenchers of succotash stew and passed around a noggin of cider.